MELISSA REEVES is a Melbourne playwright and screenwriter. She has written over twenty plays and won numerous awards. She has been closely associated with the Red Shed Company and Melbourne Workers Theatre. Her plays include *In Cahoots*, *Sweetown* (winner of the Jill Blewitt Playwrights Award), *The Spook* (winner of the Victorian Premier's Literary Award and the major Awgie), *Furious Mattress* and *Archimedes War*. She co-wrote *Who's Afraid of the Working Class*, *Fever* and *Anthem* with Patricia Cornelius, Andrew Bovell, Irine Vela and Christos Tsiolkas.

Harry Musgrove, Richie Hallal, Daniela Farinacci, Jordan Fraser-Trumble and Eva Seymour in Darebin Arts Speakeasy's Archimedes War, *2021 (Photo: Pia Johnson)*

ARCHIMEDES WAR

MELISSA REEVES

CURRENCY PRESS
The performing arts publisher

CURRENCY PLAYS

First published in 2023
by Currency Press Pty Ltd,
PO Box 2287, Strawberry Hills, NSW, 2012, Australia
enquiries@currency.com.au
www.currency.com.au

Copyright: *A legacy of trauma* © Jeff Sparrow, 2023; *Archimedes War* © Melissa Reeves, 2023.

COPYING FOR EDUCATIONAL PURPOSES

The Australian *Copyright Act 1968* (Act) allows a maximum of one chapter or 10% of this book, whichever is the greater, to be copied by any educational institution for its educational purposes provided that that educational institution (or the body that administers it) has given a remuneration notice to Copyright Agency (CA) under the Act.

For details of the CA licence for educational institutions contact CA, 12/66 Goulburn Street, Sydney, NSW, 2000; tel: within Australia 1800 066 844 toll free; outside Australia 61 2 9394 7600; fax: 61 2 9394 7601; email: memberservices@copyright.com.au.

COPYING FOR OTHER PURPOSES

Except as permitted under the Act, for example a fair dealing for the purposes of study, research, criticism or review, no part of this book may be reproduced, stored in a retrieval system, or transmitted in any form or by any means without prior written permission. All enquiries should be made to the publisher at the address above.

Any performance or public reading of *Archimedes War* is forbidden unless a licence has been received from the author or the author's agent. The purchase of this book in no way gives the purchaser the right to perform the play in public, whether by means of a staged production or a reading. All applications for public performance should be addressed to Fran Moore, fran@franmoore.com.au.

Typeset by Lucinda Naughton for Currency Press.
Cover design by Katherine Zhang for Currency Press.

Currency Press acknowledges the Traditional Owners of the Country on which we live and work. We pay our respects to all Aboriginal and Torres Strait Islander Elders, past and present.

A catalogue record for this book is available from the National Library of Australia

Contents

A legacy of trauma Jeff Sparrow	*vii*
Acknowledgements	*xiii*
ARCHIMEDES WAR	1

A legacy of trauma

This is a play about the war in Afghanistan and its consequences.

On 12 September 2001—the day after the terrorist attacks in New York—Prime Minister John Howard invoked the ANZUS Treaty for the first time ever, committing the country to fight alongside the US whatever the circumstances.

By the next month, Australian soldiers were in Afghanistan. Parliament did not formally debate the conflict until an astonishing nine years later.

Much of the media treated the commitment with an extraordinary insouciance.

'Australian military forces are joining a long-overdue fight against evil,' explained the *Sunday Telegraph*'s Piers Akerman, in a piece typical of the time. 'Is that too difficult to understand?'

By the time Australia withdrew from Afghanistan in 2021, the Costs of War project estimated the invasion had resulted in the deaths of 176,000 people, more than 45,000 of whom were civilians. Other estimates put the toll much, much higher. Close to three million people (from a nation of 38 million) fled the country; another four million became internal refugees.

As the foreign forces left, the Taliban returned. The new regime struggled to provide basic services, even before a US freeze on assets owned by Afghan banks brought financial collapse. Decades of war thus culminated in a horrific (and ongoing) humanitarian crisis.

Such were the results of the *Telegraph*'s 'fight against evil'.

In *Archimedes War*, Melissa Reeves presents us with men and women haunted by violence.

The poet Wilfred Owen knew such people.

'These are men whose minds the dead have ravished,' he wrote. 'Memory fingers in their hair of murders, multitudinous murders they once witnessed.'

The Great War, in which Owen fought and died, revealed a fundamental paradox about military conflict, one that Reeves' play explores in depth.

The hostilities of 1914 spurred, at least for a while, a kind of ecstasy among young men, who looked to war for the adventure and excitement and meaning that everyday modernity failed to provide. Something similar (albeit on a much, much smaller scale) could be said about Australia's invasion of Afghanistan. When the Greens Senator Scott Ludlam visited the country in 2008, he wrote of how, the closer he came to the front, the happier and more excited the soldiers seemed.

'I'd do this whether you paid me or not,' said one.

Reeves' character Aaron feels the same way.

'I have this stupid hankering to go back to Afghanistan,' he admits. 'The place made me so sick, but I want to go back there. Offer me a ticket, I'd be straight on the plane. What's that about eh?'

The novelist and war reporter Sebastian Junger would answer that battle offers young men a freedom they rarely experience in a world that, he says, has 'perfected the art of making people not feel necessary'.

Combat reduces life to its essence, replacing social complexities with the simplicity of violence and survival. Junger talks about the 'profound alienation of modern society' and then concludes that, 'when combat vets say that they miss the war, they might be having an entirely healthy response to life.'

In the play, Major Nelson Smith explains: 'War is the biggest, most spiritual thrill there is. Now don't get me wrong, I'm not saying it's a good thing ... I'm just saying nothing ever comes close ever again, if you survive it. Nowhere near close.'

Yet, the modern military strives to depersonalise warfare, drilling soldiers so relentlessly that, amid the noise and terror, they perform as automatically as robots. The mechanisation already apparent in the First World War facilitated that process, transforming the battlefield into a vast factory of death where men who craved chivalry and honour killed each other as if working an assembly line.

In *Archimedes War*, Connie pilots a Predator drone from an air-conditioned military base thousands of kilometres from the frontline: an experience akin to Arki's video games, albeit with real people dying.

Even frontline soldiers sometimes report finding combat strangely underwhelming.

When I researched my book *Killing: Misadventures in Violence*, I spoke to veterans from Iraq and Afghanistan who could recall the onset of a firefight and its aftermath but lacked any recollection of aiming and shooting at their enemies as the muscle memories drilled into them during basic training took over and they killed without even realising they'd done so.

By rendering violence automatic, unemotional and mechanical, the military insulates soldiers from the psychological revulsion associated with gunning down a fellow human being.

Yet many say that the absence of feeling comes, eventually, to consume them. They have killed people—sometimes many. They have done the worst things that human beings can do—and yet they have no context to assimilate acts they barely recall. The disconnect engenders a deep trauma, the sentiment that runs throughout Reeves' play.

'The thing is,' says Aaron, 'the thing you're always trying to push out of your mind, cause for all the training you do, teaching you how not to think, you do think, you can't help but think, and you think why?'

Of course, some wars raise that question more than others.

In 2008, SAS soldiers killed a Taliban leader called Mullah Noorullah in what the Australian media described as a revived version of the Vietnam-era Phoenix Program.

It was an astonishing admission, especially given how casually it was made. For Phoenix was an assassination program synonymous with the worst atrocities of the Vietnam War.

The intelligence officer Lieutenant Vincent Okamoto described it as follows:

> The normal procedure would be to go into a village and just grab someone and say, 'Where's Nguyen so-and-so?' Half the time the people were so afraid they would say anything. Then a Phoenix team would take the informant, put a sandbag over his head, poke out two holes so he could see, put commo wire around his neck like a long leash, and walk him through the village and say, 'When we go by Nguyen's house scratch your head.' Then that night Phoenix would come back, knock on the door, and say, 'April Fool, motherfucker.' Whoever answered the door would get wasted. As far as they were concerned whoever answered was a Communist, including family members.

Not coincidentally, local villagers later claimed that the assassination team targeting Mullah Noorullah also shot five children and another civilian.

In his book *Vietnam: The Australian War*, Paul Ham describes how, by 1970, Phoenix involved 'squads of wild-eyed, often drugged, Vietnamese killers roam[ing] the countryside and indiscriminately round[ing] up and tortur[ing] suspects or civilian sympathisers'.

The decision to revive that program decades later speaks volumes about the nature of the Afghan intervention.

But, from the minute they entered the country, the coalition forces relied upon collaboration with the warlords of the Northern Alliance, many of whom were notorious for their human rights abuses.

The Australian Defence Forces collaborated closely, for instance, with a man called Matiullah Khan, even bringing him to Australia for training. The *New York Times* later estimated that Matiullah earned two-and-a-half million US dollars a month through various forms of gangsterism, including extortion, robbery and drug trafficking. In response, the Australian commander explained: 'He may not be an angel but he's our guy and we should work with him.'

As early as 2008, a leaked cable quoted the British ambassador in Afghanistan explaining that the best outcome of the war would be government by an 'acceptable dictator' and that 'we should think of preparing our public opinion' to accept that.

The photogenic Hamid Karzai eventually played the dictator role, kept in power by the US despite his corruption and gangsterism. The *Washington Post* revealed that the CIA funnelled billions of dollars to Karzai's brother, a drug lord, on the basis that the occupation would collapse without the family's military support.

At around the same time, the legendary journalist Bob Woodward reported that the CIA had established its own covert army of 3000 special operatives, conducting secret assassinations in the tribal regions of Afghanistan and Pakistan.

The echoes from Vietnam should not surprise us. Unpopular counter-insurgency missions necessarily draw on the same few strategies—and produce the same results.

The Brereton report into Australian war crimes in Afghanistan exposed a military culture in which all Afghan people were seen as the enemy—so much so that experienced soldiers allegedly 'blooded' their younger comrades by instructing them to murder detainees.

A similar phenomenon took place in Vietnam, where, according to historian Nick Turse, Western soldiers adhered to what they called the 'MGR'—the 'mere gook rule'—in which 'all Vietnamese—northern and southern, adults and children, armed enemy and innocent civilians—were little more than animals, who could be killed or abused at will.'

In his 1955 *Discourses on Colonialism*, the poet and activist Aimé Cesaire spoke of 'thing-ification': the process by which imperial nations turned those they ruled into mere objects. You can't occupy another country without degrading its people: you must assert their inferiority in order to justify your power over them. In Vietnam, the foreign soldiers used the word 'gook' whereas in Afghanistan it was 'haji' but the thing-ification remained the same.

In the midst of a parlour guessing game, Aaron blurts out the question that plagues him: 'Am I a war criminal?'

Most soldiers did not personally play any role in the atrocities documented in the Brereton report. But, as the play shows, the brutality of an unnecessary war exacerbates the trauma suffered by those who fought in it.

Cesaire made a further argument—and one well worth considering in respect of Afghanistan.

He insisted that the European societies of his day were, whether they knew it or not, fundamentally affected by their investment in colonial violence.

'[A]t the end of all these treaties that have been violated,' he argued, 'all these punitive expeditions that have been tolerated, all these prisoners who have been tied up and interrogated, all these patriots who have been tortured, at the end of all the racial pride that has been encouraged, all the boastfulness that has been displayed, a poison has been instilled into the veins of Europe and, slowly but surely, the continent proceeds toward savagery.'

The conflict in Afghanistan lasted five times as long as the First World War and more than three times longer than the Second World War.

What toxins did it leave behind?

In 2019, defence analyst Clive Williams casually explained that 'the real reason [for Australian participation in Afghanistan] is of course to show we are a willing ANZUS and Western alliance partner in order to be well regarded by the US and receive the defence and intelligence benefits that go with active membership of the Five-Eyes relationship.'

His breezy 'of course' implied that insiders had always understood the intervention as nothing to do with Afghanistan itself (dismissed by Williams as 'of little strategic importance to Australia') but rather an effort to cement closer military ties with America.

Indeed, the ten billion dollars Canberra devoted to the occupation of Afghanistan might be seen as a precursor to the $368 billion allocated to nuclear submarines under the new AUKUS agreement: a deal important to defence strategists less because of the vessels themselves and more because, like the Afghan war, it draws the US into closer military ties with Australia.

Reeves' play depicts war as never-ending, a nightmare her characters live over and over again.

In that respect, it offers a warning.

The vast investment in AUKUS necessarily comes at the expense of other allocations, far dwarfing any commitment to, say, addressing climate change. It also locks Australia into future American wars, at a time when tensions between the US and China have never been greater.

Archimedes War invites us to think about Afghanistan and its legacy. Will we break the cycle of trauma or will that conflict pave the way for even greater catastrophes to come?

Jeff Sparrow

Jeff Sparrow is a writer, editor and journalist. He teaches at the Centre for Advancing Journalism at the University of Melbourne.

Acknowledgements

Many voices have contributed to the development of *Archimedes War*. I'd like to thank Susie Dee, who directed the premier production in 2021 at the Northcote Townhall Arts Centre, and the cast and creative team—Daniela Farinacci, Jim Russell, Richie Hallal, Harry Musgrove, Jordan Fraser-Trumble, Eva Seymour, Romanie Harper, Bethany J Fellows, Ian Moorhead and Lisa Mibus. I'd also like to thank Chris Mead who dramaturged the play over much of its development. *Archimedes War* was workshopped at Playwrighting Australia (now Australian Plays Transform) and presented as part of the Cybec readings at the MTC, and showcased at the National Play Festival in 2016. Thank you to Iain Sinclair, Tanya Dickson, Amber McMahon, Tom Conroy, Steve LeMarquand, Danielle Cormack, Anna Samson, Aljin Abella, Maria Theodorakis, Colin Moody, Mark Winter, Anna McGahon, Alice Fleming, Rodney Afif, Harry Tseng, Anthony Gooley, Osamah Sami, Darcy Brown, Kath Tonkin, and Sahil Saluja. Thank you also to Kate Reeves, Patricia Cornelius, Andrew Bovell, Cath Mckinnon, Tim Coldwell, Lenny Reeves, Hoagy Reeves, Louis Carlin, and the Literature Board of the Australia Council.

Harry Musgrove in Darebin Arts Speakeasy's Archimedes War, *2021 (Photo: Pia Johnson)*

Archimedes War was first produced by Darebin Arts Speakeasy at Northcote Town Hall, on the lands of the Wurundjeri Woiwurrung people of the Kulin Nation, Melbourne, on 25 November 2021, with the following cast:

ARKI	Harry Musgrove
RAY/SAYF/BANQUO	Richie Hallal
CAROLINE/NADIA/FLEANCE	Daniela Farinacci
NELSON/FIRST MURDERER	Jim Russell
AARON/SECOND MURDERER	Jordan Fraser-Trumble
LILY/CONNIE	Eva Seymour

Director, Susie Dee
Set and video design, Romanie Harper
Set and costume design, Bethany J Fellows
Lighting design, Lisa Mibus
Sound design, Ian Moorhead

CHARACTERS

ARKI, fifteen-year-old boy
RAY, Arki's psychiatrist
CAROLINE, Arki's mother
NADIA, runs an Afghan restaurant
SAYF, Nadia's younger brother, early thirties
NELSON, an Army Public Relations Officer
AARON, an Australian soldier, early thirties
LILY, married to AARON
CONNIE, eighteen-year-old Australian soldier
BANQUO
FLEANCE
FIRST MURDERER
SECOND MURDERER

NOTES

The actor playing Nelson should also play First Murderer; the actor playing Ray should also play Banquo; the actor playing Aaron should also play Second Murderer; and the actor playing Caroline should also play Fleance.

For a cast of six performers other possible doubles are:

Caroline/Nadia

Ray/Sayfe

Lily/Connie

SCENE ONE

ARKI, *fifteen years old, is seeing a psychiatrist,* RAY.

RAY: Lonely?
ARKI: Seven.
RAY: Excited?
ARKI: Sometimes.
RAY: Out of ten.
ARKI: Six.
RAY: Nervous?
ARKI: Seven.
RAY: Irritable?
ARKI: Seven.
RAY: Angry?
ARKI: Six.
RAY: Feelings of pleasure …?
ARKI: Well I—
RAY: Just try and put it out of ten.
ARKI: Seven.
RAY: How's your sleep?
ARKI: Okay.
RAY: You nod off as soon as your head touches the pillow?
ARKI: I can lie there for a bit.
RAY: Do you wake up in the night?
ARKI: Sometimes.
RAY: Bad dreams?
ARKI: Sometimes.
RAY: What do you dream about?
ARKI: I can't remember.
RAY: Try and remember some of your dreams for me, okay?

    ARKI *nods.*

Do you like school Arki?

    ARKI *shrugs in assent.*

Tell me about what happened last Tuesday.

ARKI: I got angry.
RAY: What about?
ARKI: I dunno.
RAY: What were you thinking about …?

>ARKI *laughs involuntarily.*

You find it funny?
ARKI: No.
RAY: It is sort of funny.
ARKI: I don't find it funny.
RAY: I can see why you'd find it funny.
ARKI: I don't …
>I had a headache.

RAY: Uh-huh.

>ARKI *clams up.*

What class was it?
ARKI: English.
RAY: With—

>*He checks his notes.*

Mr Benalli.

>ARKI *says nothing.*

What do you think about Mr Benalli?
ARKI: I don't think anything about him.
RAY: So what was happening in class that day?
ARKI: We were reading *Macbeth* … And Mr Benalli said for me to read the murderer, but I didn't know where we were up to cause I hadn't been following really, so the girl next to me pointed out the passage, it was this speech about how Banquo's lying dead in a ditch, this guy's hacked him to death, and he has twenty bloody gashes in his head. Anyway … I said I didn't want to read.
RAY: Why?
ARKI: I found the passage offensive … And everyone laughed, and Mr Benalli comes over and he puts on this stupid voice, goes, you find it offensive?
RAY: And then what happened?
ARKI: I can't remember.

RAY: But you know that you hit him?
ARKI: Gabriel said it was more of a push.
RAY: Why were you so upset by the play?
ARKI: I wasn't upset. I just don't get why we have to be reading about this weak arsehole killer, and his murdering old bag of a wife. It pisses me off that people have such a problem with combat games on Xbox and PS4s and meanwhile Shakespeare gets off on writing serial killer porn.
RAY: Okay, well they're strong opinions. Something you could talk about with the class maybe, or with your teacher.

    ARKI *says nothing.*

Do you get on well with the other kids at school?
ARKI: Yep.
RAY: Are you in a particular group at school? Are you like, in the jocks, or the dags, or the brains?
ARKI: I don't know what you mean by those categories.
RAY: Okay …
    Shall we bring your mum back in?

    ARKI *stares at* RAY.

ARKI: I see weird things.
RAY: What sort of things?
ARKI: I dunno, sort of visions … you know … of dead people. People that have been shot with machine guns, and blown up with hand grenades.
RAY: Do you know any of these people?

    ARKI *shakes his head.*

They're not family members, or fellow students—?
ARKI: I know where they're from. They're from a game that I play. *Combat Mission: America at War.*
RAY: You see dead characters from your game?

    ARKI *says nothing.*

Can you see them now?
ARKI: Yeah …
RAY: Where?
ARKI: Over there.

    ARKI *motions with his head, not wanting to look.*

RAY: Over where?
ARKI: By the window.

>RAY *looks at the window.*

There's a guy. He's missing his face.

>ARKI *quickly glances over and back again.*

He's gone.

>ARKI *is distressed.*

RAY: It's alright Arki.
It's alright.
Were you seeing any of these … apparitions in Mr Benalli's English class?
ARKI: There were heaps of them. All round the room. There was a guy with his ear ripped off, and blood all coming down, he was sitting at Mr. Benalli's desk, and there was a guy who looked like he had been shot while he was trying to get out the door, and there was a guy with his legs blown off. He was sitting in Eugene's seat.
RAY: What do they look like?
ARKI: Have you played any games?
RAY: Yeah.
ARKI: What do you play?
RAY: *Team Fortress.*
ARKI: Oh yeah that's a cool game. Yeah well they just look like that, like game characters. But they're good ones. They look really real.
RAY: Did you kill them?
ARKI: I don't know for certain that I killed them, those exact ones.
RAY: But you've killed ones like them?
ARKI: Yeah.
RAY: How do you kill them?
ARKI: With your gun mainly, or with a hand grenade, or if they get too close, you have to use your knife that you have hidden in your sock.

>RAY *looks at his shoes.* ARKI *sees him looking.*

It's just in the game. I'm not a psychopath.
RAY: Okay.

>RAY *gets up to let Arki's mum* CAROLINE *into the room.*

Arki, would you mind waiting outside while I have a chat to your mum?

ARKI *goes and sits outside the room.*

CAROLINE: Did he tell you why he hit his teacher?
RAY: I'm getting a bit of a picture.
CAROLINE: He won't tell me anything at the moment.
RAY: How often is he playing his computer games?
CAROLINE: His games. He's always playing them. He's always on them. He's got so many different gadgets, you can't keep tabs on them all. I wondered if it might be something to do with them. But I just thought most kids are playing them nonstop, he says they are, he says he's nothing special.
RAY: Arki said he sometimes has bad dreams.
CAROLINE: They're worse than bad dreams. He wakes up in a sweat.
RAY: I think maybe it would be useful, Caroline, if you could come to a session, and we could talk, the three of us.
CAROLINE: Of course.
RAY: I'd like to canvas any events in Arki's life that may be causing him distress.
CAROLINE: Okay.
RAY: Arki's been having visual hallucinations.
CAROLINE: What?
RAY: It's alright—
CAROLINE: What's wrong with him?
RAY: I'm not sure, but you need to relax, take Arki back to school—
CAROLINE: He's suspended from school. That's why we're here.
RAY: Of course. I'm sorry. Look I understand you want immediate answers, but it doesn't always work like that … And to be honest, Arki's case has some … curious features—
CAROLINE: Like what?
RAY: I'd like to consult some of my colleagues.
CAROLINE: You're freaking me out.
RAY: That's the last thing I want to do.
CAROLINE: Tell me.
RAY: Arki appears to be suffering from a mental condition that I don't see how he could have.

CAROLINE: What do you mean, couldn't have?
RAY: The symptoms he is exhibiting happen pretty much exclusively to soldiers who have fought in a war.

SCENE TWO

At Lily and Aaron's house, LILY *sits in the lounge room.* AARON *enters in uniform with all of his army bags. They hug. The air is full of nervous excitement.*

LILY: Wait. Wait. I've got champagne.
AARON: Champagne eh?
LILY: Moët.
AARON: Okay.

    LILY *disappears and comes back with a bottle of champagne. She opens it. They laugh.*

LILY: To you.
AARON: To you.
LILY: To you alive.

    They drink.

AARON: You good?
LILY: Yeah I'm good. You good?
AARON: Yeah I'm good ...
    How many bottles of this stuff have you got?
LILY: Three.

    AARON *laughs. They drink.*

AARON: Taxi driver was from Iraq.
LILY: You're kidding.
AARON: He says where were you? Were you in Fallujah? I said nah. He said were you in Bagdad? I said I wasn't in Iraq mate ...

    They laugh, slightly awkward. They drink.

    Where's Chloe?
LILY: She's asleep.
AARON: I thought she might be at your mum's.
LILY: No she's asleep. In her room ...
    I've got a new tattoo.

AARON: Yeah. Where?
LILY: Guess.
AARON: Um, I've forgotten where the other one is.

Lily's old tattoo is plain for all to see, on her arm.

LILY: Get stuffed.

AARON starts rummaging in one of his bags.

AARON: So where's the new one?

AARON gets out a small cloth package. He gives her the package. She unwraps it. In the package is the most beautiful filigree gold Afghan necklace. LILY *holds it up to look at it.*

LILY: Oh god, Aaron. It's beautiful.
AARON: Let me.

He takes the necklace and puts it around her neck but his hands are shaking so much he can't do it up.

LILY: You alright?
AARON: Tiny little catch.

He keeps trying without success.

Shitful thing … Come over to the light.

They move closer to the light as an awkward unit. LILY *laughs. He still can't do it up.*

LILY: I can do it.
AARON: I can do it.

He finally gets it done up.

So where's this tattoo?
LILY: I'm not telling.
AARON: Small of your back?

He looks at the small of her back.

Where's this new tattoo?
LILY: Haven't you found it yet?
AARON: Back of your calf?
LILY: Nah.
AARON: Under your ear?

LILY: Yeah. I got little bolts put there …

They laugh.

It's here.

He looks at where she's pointing.

AARON: Where? In your pubes?
LILY: Pretty much.
AARON: Crazy girl.

He kisses her new tattoo. She laughs. They laugh. A baby starts crying.

LILY: I'll get her.
AARON: No I'll get her.

He exits.

LILY: You gonna change her?
AARON: [*off*] Yeah, I'll change her.

Eva Seymour and Jordan Fraser-Trumble in Darebin Arts Speakeasy's Archimedes War, *2021 (Photo: Pia Johnson)*

SCENE THREE

CAROLINE *is with an Army Public Relations Officer—Major* NELSON SMITH. *He is dressed in uniform. He stares at her like she's a loony.*

NELSON: I'm not really clear what you think I can do to help … Are you looking for some kind of compensation?
CAROLINE: No.
NELSON: I was going to say. You're drawing a mighty long bow.

No-one speaks for a moment.

You read the papers I take it. You know we're at war?
CAROLINE: I know that. In Iraq and—
NELSON: That one's finished, that one.
CAROLINE: And … Afghanistan.
NELSON: Yeah. So young men, and women, frighteningly young, go and fight overseas for their country and war is a very stressful, very boring, at times … very frightening, very dangerous occupation and they come back home, and most people they meet, don't have a clue, whether there's a war on, or which one's going on at the present moment, and some of them, a small proportion, get sick. Get mentally sick because that high octane life as a soldier serving overseas has overstimulated their brains, this is just my take on it, don't quote me on this, and they can't calm down, they're treating this lovely civilian coffee-sipping, celebrity-spotting life like they are still out on a mission, they are still in daily fear of their life, that they could be blown up by a roadside bomb, or shot dead by a sniper, or god forbid, taken down by someone they trust, while they're cleaning their teeth, or putting out the rubbish, they get shot and killed by someone whom they regarded as an ally. Now forgive me if I sound slightly bemused when I say that this is a profoundly different thing to a boy playing too many video games.

   CAROLINE *takes this in.*

CAROLINE: I get that. That's fine. All I want to know is how the Army deals with it.
NELSON: The Army has a duty of care to all its soldiers, and it responds

to any mental problems they may have developed through working for the Army in any capacity, with the appropriate psychiatric care, and monetary support.

CAROLINE *doesn't say anything for a moment.*

CAROLINE: Thank you for seeing me.
NELSON: Now you're pissed off.
CAROLINE: I'm not pissed off.
NELSON: Look ma'am.
CAROLINE: Caroline.
NELSON: Caroline. I don't want to be mean to you. I'm sorry your boy's sick. I've got kids of my own. I've got a nineteen-year-old, and a twenty-two-year-old. It's a life sentence, parenthood, isn't it? You worry about them from the moment they're born. I'm sure you and your husband are worried sick.
CAROLINE: I don't have a husband.
NELSON: Well that makes it difficult, doesn't it.
CAROLINE: It's not that difficult.
NELSON: I'm sure it's substantially more difficult.
CAROLINE: I'm used to it now. It's fine.
NELSON: I can see you're putting on a brave face.
CAROLINE: No I'm not.
NELSON: Whatever … Look, personally, I think this psychiatrist is barking up the wrong tree, but Kara at the front desk might have some pamphlets that could help you a bit more than I can.

CAROLINE *starts to leave.*

You know, it's quite an unforgiving task, being the public face of the Army.
CAROLINE: I'm sure it is.
NELSON: I don't want you to get the wrong idea.
CAROLINE: What do you mean by the wrong idea?
NELSON: There is an unfortunate, enduring perception that being in the Army makes you into some kind of robot.
CAROLINE: Uh-huh.
NELSON: Let me tell you soldiers are some of the most interesting, well-read, deep-thinking, funny, passionate and unique people around. More interesting for example than footballers. Even footballers who

have been on the Kokoda track. I wouldn't barrack for any football team who goes to the Kokoda track to walk in a bit of mud and have a bonding session. Give me a break.

CAROLINE: I love the footy.

NELSON: Well, I'm not saying the game's not entertaining.

CAROLINE: I know a lot of players. They come to my gym.

NELSON: You have a gym?

CAROLINE: It's not my gym. I just work there.

NELSON: Well you know what they say. At any rate. When a player does yet another of their endless anterior cruciate ligaments? A soldier has fallen. I'm sorry this is a personal bugbear of mine, but, how dare they? This bloke's got a bung knee, or a bit of concussion at the most, he hasn't stepped on an IED and been blown to bits. I can't bear it.

Let me meet your son. Let me have a talk to him. What's his name?

CAROLINE: Arki.

NELSON: Arki? What's that short for?

CAROLINE: Archimedes.

NELSON: Yeah well I'll have a chat to Archimedes and see if we can't sort this out.

SCENE FOUR

NELSON *and* ARKI *are out for a milkshake.*

NELSON: So you like playing war games?

ARKI: I don't call them that.

NELSON: What do you call them?

ARKI: First-person shooter. Combat games.

NELSON: Sounds like war.

ARKI: Yeah, well that's the scenery.

NELSON: Just the scenery?

ARKI: It's more about the skills you know, than the story.

I mean, sure, it's there, in the background. Explosions, and … snipers … and … stuff.

NELSON *takes out a cigarette.*

NELSON: You want one?

ARKI: No thank you.

NELSON: Good. That was a test … Smoking is bad for you. What sort of gun do you have?
ARKI: An AK-twelve.
NELSON: The Ruskie. Why'd you pick that?
ARKI: It was affordable, and it was the right weapon for the terrain I'm in. I needed a reliable, medium range assault rifle.
NELSON: They've got a kick like a mule.
ARKI: They've been upgraded for less recoil.
NELSON: I'll believe that when I see it.
ARKI: I've also got a sniper rifle, a Dragunov.
NELSON: What is it with you and the Ruskies?
ARKI: I've customised it with an extended mag, and a sight with an enhanced zoom, and I've got nearly enough points for an infrared scope which is really cool. It highlights enemy targets in white, and you get a better shot at the head.
NELSON: Ever thought about joining the Army?
ARKI: Not really.
NELSON: Any of your family ever been in the Army? Or the Navy?
ARKI: Nup.
NELSON: Air Force?
ARKI: Nup.

NELSON smokes.

NELSON: Milkshake okay?
ARKI: Yeah it's good, thanks.

They are silent for a moment.

NELSON: You want to ask me anything?
ARKI: No.
NELSON: You sure? You've got a real live Major here. I was in Timor. And the Solomon Islands. I fought in Iraq.

ARKI can't think of anything to ask.

I thought you would want to ask me what it's like to kill someone. Like kill someone for real, on the field, not just in a game.
ARKI: Oh right.
NELSON: You want to ask me that? What it's like to kill someone?
ARKI: Okay.

NELSON: How old are you?
ARKI: Fifteen.
NELSON: Which version should I give you? Should I give you the G, the PG, the M or the R?
ARKI: The M?
NELSON: The M. Some violence, sexual references, adult concepts. You kids are growing up fast these days. I'm gonna give you the R …

    He leans in close ...

It's very satisfying. In my experience. Just my experience, mind you. It's a subjective thing. You're shitting your pants in terror, the guns are so loud you can't hear yourself think, you're dressed up in so much gear, you feel like Michelin Man, and all you know is it's you against them, and when you pot one, and you got them and they didn't get you, you feel triumphant, you feel like a conqueror. You're hardly a man, when you join the Army, a year older than you, sixteen, seventeen, and you're plying your trade at the world's oldest profession, cause it's not prostitution like they say, it's war. The prostitutes only came cause there was a big war on, and there were lots of soldiers wanting to … War is the biggest, most spiritual thrill there is. Now don't get me wrong, I'm not saying it's a good thing Arki. I'm just saying nothing ever comes close ever again, if you survive it. Nowhere near close. Now you, all you're doing is make-believe. Worshipping at the altar, maybe, but that's all. You haven't killed anybody. Have you?

ARKI: Nah.
NELSON: You've got nothing to be worried about, or stress your mind about.
    And you shouldn't be worrying your mother in this way. Alright?
ARKI: Yep.
NELSON: She's got enough on her plate.
ARKI: Yeah.
NELSON: Don't be a pussy.

SCENE FIVE

At Caroline and Arki's house. CAROLINE *drinks from a glass of wine.* ARKI *plays on his phone. She looks at him.*

ARKI: I'm just looking at my messages.

ARKI *remains absorbed in his phone.*

CAROLINE: You know what I think.
ARKI: Yes, and I have stopped.
CAROLINE: Not just the war one. All of them.
ARKI: What, you're gonna cut me off completely from society? No phone? No internet?
CAROLINE: No, not no internet. No games.

ARKI *ignores her.*

I think they're too dangerous for you. Like alcohol is a problem for some people, and some people can cope … with a bit … you know …

She drinks some wine. ARKI *sniggers meanly.* CAROLINE *chooses to ignore him.*

It's like you can't cope with video games.
ARKI: That's just bullshit.
CAROLINE: What if these games are like rewiring your brain, and desensitising you to violence, and triggering violent impulses you can't control—
ARKI: God Mum. You find a few websites, and you think you've got the whole thing worked out. You look up Doctor Google, and now you're an expert.
CAROLINE: Have you read about the kids that play for three days straight and then just fall out of their chair, dead?

I'm not saying you're like this Arki, but one boy, in Alabama, killed his parents when they tried to stop him playing.

ARKI *looks at her malevolently.*

All they said was you better get off your game now, son, and he picked up a hunting knife and he killed them, father first, then his mother. Why they had a hunting knife just lying around, I don't know. That

seems a bit fucking irresponsible. But if that's what violent games can do—
ARKI: What was he playing?
CAROLINE: I don't know what he was playing.
ARKI: Well that seems quite relevant Mum, to your argument. What if he was just playing *Mario Kart*?
CAROLINE: What if he was?
ARKI: Well then it wouldn't be about the game then would it?
CAROLINE: Which one's *Mario Kart*?
ARKI: You're talking like we don't think about this stuff. I can show you websites where kids talk all about the games, and review them, and talk about how violent they are, how graphic they are, rate them out of twenty on a whole lot of criteria, like the story, and the characters, whether they're sexist or not. There's this whole dialogue going on that you know nothing about.
CAROLINE: And have you gone on that website and talked about what's happening to you?
ARKI: No.
CAROLINE: Why don't you?
ARKI: I don't want to.
CAROLINE: Why don't you?
ARKI: I just don't want to.
CAROLINE: Talk to your internet friends.
ARKI: Mum! Shut up! Just shut up!
CAROLINE: Don't get so fucking angry.
ARKI: I get angry cause you just go on and on at me.

> *Pause.*

CAROLINE: So what are you going to do tonight?

> ARKI *says nothing.*

Will you play games?

> *Pause.*

ARKI: I dunno. I might play *FIFA*.

> CAROLINE *nods.*

Or *Assassin's Creed.*
CAROLINE: *Assassin's Creed.* What happens in that?

ARKI: It's just pirates and stuff like that.

   CAROLINE looks suspicious.

There's killing in it, but honestly, it's tame.

CAROLINE: Do we see blood?

ARKI: Not really.

CAROLINE: Do they die graphically?

ARKI: No.

CAROLINE: Well, how do they die?

ARKI: They just die.

CAROLINE: How do they die?

ARKI: They … sort of … grunt, and fall over.

   They laugh.

CAROLINE: It's still killing, Arki …

ARKI: So's *Bugs Bunny*!

CAROLINE: What about the one with the blocks and you make your own roller-coaster … You used to love that.

   ARKI says nothing.

I don't know if I should leave you by yourself.

ARKI: I'm fine.

   Neither of them say anything for a moment.

I'm fine Mum.

   They are quiet for a moment.

Where are you going anyway?

CAROLINE: I've got a date.

SCENE SIX

LILY *and* AARON *sit together in a restaurant called Nights in Kabul. There's a carafe of wine at their table. The atmosphere is tense.*

LILY: Do you want a glass of wine?

AARON: Sure.

   They say nothing for a moment.

LILY: I'm sorry Aaron. We should have gone French or Italian, or Mexican or something …

AARON *says nothing.*

I'm sorry if I've upset you.

AARON *says nothing.*

I thought I might have made a mistake when I told you what the restaurant was called …

I was going to text you, but I didn't. I was going to lie and say that it had closed down.

AARON: You were going to lie, were you?

NADIA *arrives to give them wine glasses and take their order.*

NADIA: Are you ready to order?
LILY: Um …

She glances at AARON. *He gives away nothing.*

The dolma …
NADIA: Dolma yes …
LILY: And the … ashak.
NADIA: I'm sorry, we haven't got that tonight.
LILY: Okay.

LILY *looks at the menu but her heart isn't in it.*

NADIA: You could have bamya.
LILY: What's that got in it?
NADIA: Okra with tomato and onion.
LILY: Okra. Do you like okra?

AARON *shrugs.*

Okay. The okra, and the eggplant … and um … some meat … the kebabs … and the green salad … Thank you.

NADIA *leaves.* AARON *drinks some of his wine.*

So … did you lift some weights?
AARON: Yeah.
LILY: And did you catch up with Lozzer and Bix?
AARON: Yeah.
LILY: I took Chloe to the swimming pool, and she really liked it.
AARON: Are you some sort of retard?

LILY *says nothing for a moment.*

LILY: I just didn't think ...
AARON: You always were a space cadet.
LILY: Okay okay ...
AARON: Why in your wildest dreams would you think I would want to come and eat here?
LILY: I don't know.
AARON: That's cause there's no good reason.
LILY: I'm sorry ... I thought, I don't know. That we could ... share something.
AARON: Share what?
LILY: I dunno. Just, you know, the food.
AARON: I didn't eat this food. Over there. I ate normal food.
LILY: Okay.
AARON: You're a moron.
LILY: Can you stop insulting me?
AARON: Do you think I want to eat these people's food?
LILY: I don't get this Aaron. You weren't fighting these people. You were fighting the Taliban.
AARON: Keep your voice down.
LILY: These people weren't the enemy.
AARON: Well they look very like them.
LILY: But they're not. Are they?
AARON: I didn't say they were. I said they looked like them.
LILY: You were helping people like this. If I told them what you have been doing for the last five years they'd probably give us our dinner for free.
AARON: You are so ignorant.
LILY: You're a shithead.

    LILY *is upset.*

It's just a restaurant.
AARON: You think I want to spend a fun night, constantly being reminded of what an Afghan looks like, as if I needed reminding. For god's sake I can't think of a more tactless, more mindless, more ignorant act. What do you think I've been doing? Going on a nice trip and seeing the sights, I'm not a tourist Lily.

    He slugs down his wine and pours himself another. NADIA *and her younger brother* SAYF *are watching them.*

LILY: I know that.

AARON: Give me a few years at home just doing normal things before I have to revisit all this shit. Why can't we have fish and chips on the pier. What the fuck is wrong with that?

    LILY *grows more upset.*

Oh cry. That's right. Cry.

    NADIA *brings over cutlery to their table.*

AARON: Thank you. What's your name?

NADIA: Nadia.

AARON: That's a lovely name. Where are you from Nadia?

NADIA: Kandehar.

    NADIA *gives* LILY *her cutlery.*

LILY: Thanks.

    NADIA *leaves.*

    AARON *picks up his cigarettes and goes outside.*

    LILY *just sits.* NADIA *brings over another carafe of white wine.*

    AARON *comes back inside.*

AARON: I'm sorry.

LILY: It's fine.

AARON: I overreacted.

LILY: It's fine.

AARON: I'm sorry.

    They don't speak for a moment. LILY *pours* AARON *a glass of wine.*

I'm a jerk.

    He has a sip of wine.

LILY: No it's fine.

AARON: I shouldn't have been a jerk …

LILY: Don't worry about it.

AARON: It's just … you don't seem to be very sensitive at the moment. You know what I mean? I've never thought of you as insensitive, I know you're a bit crazy or whatever, you get my name tattooed in your pubes, you buy mini sunglasses for the baby or whatever, but lately you've just been making the wrong call every time. You say you wanna watch a movie, you turn on *Zero Dark Thirty*—

LILY: That's bullshit.

AARON: You say shall I download a series for us to watch, I go yeah, thinking you'll get some sexy vampire thing, or a political thriller, or something and we can cuddle on the couch and watch it together, but what do you get? *Generation Kill. Generation Kill*—

LILY: That wasn't me.

AARON: [*loudly*] What the fuck is wrong with your head? I don't want to think about the war and you're jamming it down my throat all the time.

    SAYF *comes over because of the noise.*

SAYF: Is everything alright here?

AARON: Yep.

SAYF: Maybe just keep your voice down a bit sir.

    AARON *nods.*

    The other customers, you know …

    AARON *says nothing.* SAYF *walks away.*

AARON: [*under his breath*] Haji fuck.

LILY: What did you say?

    AARON *says nothing.*

I didn't get *Generation Kill*. You watched that with Craig.

AARON: Whatever.

LILY: I got *Boardwalk Empire*. You didn't like it.

AARON: Yeah well I didn't want to watch some shitty historical costume drama.

SCENE SEVEN

ARKI *plays* Combat Mission, *multiplayer. He is very good. Very quick. Very concentrated. He's smiling.*

ARKI: Alright … head to the train. Circles closing … I marked some crates, you take gold, I'll take blue. Fuck yes, sniper. Alright then let's compare K/D ratios bro … yeah exactly. Get your shields up Imma bait this guy. Nice, killstreaks coming upppppp …

SCENE EIGHT

LILY *and* AARON *are still at the restaurant.*

AARON: I love you.
LILY: I love you too.
AARON: I love you … I really love you.
LILY: I love you too.
AARON: I love you.
LILY: Let's go.
AARON: Okay …
    I love you for ever and ever.
LILY: I love you too.
AARON: I love you so much.
LILY: Shall we get the bill?

>LILY *looks around to ask for the bill.*

AARON: What about the entertainment?
LILY: I don't think there is any.
AARON: There's always entertainment.
LILY: I don't think so.
AARON: Whirling dervishes. I saw this pack of whirling dervishes in— argh some place. Have you ever seen a dervish?
LILY: No.

>AARON *gets up.*

Oh no Aaron, don't.

>*He lifts his arms up into the air, and starts to spin very slowly. He tilts his head to the side.*

AARON: They tilt their head to the side. Like a … Like a I don't know what.

>LILY *laughs a little.* AARON *closes his eyes.*

And their beautiful colourful skirts fan out … like a big tent.
LILY: I think you should sit down.

>AARON *starts spinning a little faster.*

AARON: Argh Lily. You should try this.

He spins faster ... SAYF *and* NADIA *emerge from the kitchen to watch.*

It's like a ride at the Royal Show.

He spins really fast ... *He stops. He looks like he might be sick.*

SCENE NINE

ARKI *is asleep in his bed.*
He screams.
CAROLINE *comes in.*

CAROLINE: Shh, it's alright ... it's alright.

ARKI *starts to calm down.*

It's alright ...

She holds him.

Come and I'll make you a hot chocolate.

ARKI *follows her into the kitchen.* NELSON *is sitting on the couch in the lounge room.*

You remember Nelson?
NELSON: How are you champ?

SCENE TEN

SAYF *tidies up the restaurant.* NADIA *watches.*

SAYF: What a prick. Spews up all over the floor, and what does he do? Nothing. Does he give us an extra twenty bucks for the trouble he caused? Nah. Nothing. Thanks mate. Thanks a million mate. Comes here and eats our food, and looks down his nose at us. Talks so loudly all the other customers leave. Treats his girlfriend like shit. Did you see that?
NADIA: Yep.
SAYF: What's he want to come here for anyway?
NADIA: He was in Afghanistan.
SAYF: Do you think I didn't get that? The whole restaurant knew that.
NADIA: I s'pose he was messed up by the war.

SAYF: So what? Who isn't?
NADIA: Forget about it.

    SAYF *finishes mopping.*

SAYF: Shit!
NADIA: What?
SAYF: Look.
NADIA: What?
SAYF: The sword. He's souvenired the sword.
NADIA: You're kidding.
SAYF: No. Look. It's gone.
NADIA: Where was it?
SAYF: There. There. It was hanging right up there.
NADIA: Are you sure?
SAYF: Of course I'm sure.
NADIA: That's terrible.
SAYF: Classic.
NADIA: But, how could we not notice?
SAYF: Looting fucking drunken Aussie prick.
NADIA: Must have put it down his pants.
SAYF: It wouldn't fit down his pants. It's huge … Don't you remember it?
NADIA: I remember it, the big gold sword.
SAYF: Bronze. A big bronze sword, with engraved writing in Aramaic on the hilt.
NADIA: Yeah, I remember it. You bought it from Cash Converters in Preston.
SAYF: So what?
NADIA: So nothing.
SAYF: It still meant a lot to me.
NADIA: Yeah I know.
SAYF: It was very old, Nadia.
NADIA: Why are you having a go at me?
SAYF: I'm not having a go at you.
NADIA: I didn't take it.
SAYF: I didn't say you took it. You just don't seem very upset.
NADIA: I am upset. I'm very upset.
SAYF: Someone has just stolen an extremely valuable item from us.
NADIA: I know.

SCENE ELEVEN

Eleven A (The following parts of this scene intercut)
AARON *is talking to* LILY *in the middle of the night. He holds a huge bronze sword.*

AARON: The thing is, the thing you're always trying to push out of your mind, cause for all the training you do, teaching you how not to think, you do think, you can't help but think, and you think why? Why? Why have they sent me here to get shot at?

> LILY *nods. He's never talked to her about the war before.*

Like a cartoon, Lil. Like Homer Simpson. Doh.

Even after three tours I'd think it ... Even the thickest, dumbest blokes in the company, even the morons with brains like wombats, like Bevan Cledder, and Craig Taylor, they think it, that they are a rabbit in a trap, and why? They have been cast in a horror movie and why?

> *He stares at her. They sit in silence.*

LILY: Like having a baby.
AARON: Having a baby?
LILY: Don't worry it's stupid.
AARON: No, say it.
LILY: Well I felt a bit like that when I was having Chloe, you remember when I had the shower, they gave me a little break and I took a shower, and I didn't want to come back, I felt like I had got myself into something and I couldn't get out of it, there was no way out of it, except something that was unbearable, something I couldn't do.

> *They don't say anything for a moment.*

I mean it wasn't life threatening.
AARON: Well it could've been.
LILY: I'm not comparing it to war—
AARON: No I get it. You're right. I get it.

> *Eleven B*
>
> CAROLINE, NELSON *and* ARKI *appear. They are playing Monopoly*

at two in the morning at Arki's house. They are all very tired.
CAROLINE: I'll give you Bond Street for White Chapel Road.
NELSON: Nup.
CAROLINE: Oh come on.
NELSON: No.
CAROLINE: You've got Regent Street.
NELSON: Yeah, and Arki's got Oxford.
CAROLINE: He'll trade with you.
ARKI: No I won't.
CAROLINE: I want to start building.
NELSON: That's what we all want.
CAROLINE: You've got hotels. And houses. Both of you. You're both doing fine.

NELSON *shrugs.*

Oh come on. Just swap it. I'm offering you Bond Street.
NELSON: I don't want to.
CAROLINE: Please.
NELSON: Why should I enable you to get a full set so you can start building houses that I'll have to pay rent for?
CAROLINE: You're a capitalist bastard.
NELSON: That's the fucking game.
CAROLINE: Don't swear in front of Arki.
ARKI: I don't care.
CAROLINE: This is a first date Nelson. You're meant to be showing your best side. Your sense of generosity, say. Not the fact you're stubbornly competitive.
NELSON: I'm not generous. I am competitive.

They are all silent for a moment. ARKI *yawns.*

Do you want to go to bed Arki?
ARKI: Nup.
CAROLINE: It's very late Arki. Why don't you go hop into bed.

ARKI *shakes his head.*

Eleven C

SAYF *is playing guitar softly to himself.*

Eleven D

AARON and LILY are still in bed. AARON has picked up the sword and is idly doing a few martial poses.

AARON: Do you know what the ancient Greeks did when they returned home from war?

LILY shakes her head.

They took it seriously … They had these rituals, you know, purification rituals for the warrior …

LILY listens.

No sex.

LILY says nothing.

And the Indians, the American Indians, they'd go and live in a special room in the house, by themselves, for months, wouldn't eat any pepper or salt … Some shaman guy would chant special songs.

LILY nods.

The girl soldiers of Sierra Leone get washed with a special soap …

They are quiet a moment.

Lily, if I—

LILY: No, don't say it. You're going to be fine.
AARON: I've got to say it. I've got to talk about it.
LILY: You're going to be fine.

Eleven E

At Arki's house, CAROLINE *surveys the mountains of cash and property amassed by* NELSON *and* ARKI. *She takes one of Nelson's smokes.*

ARKI: What are you doing?
CAROLINE: I'm just having a smoke.
ARKI: Mum.
CAROLINE: Shut up.
ARKI: Whose go is it?
NELSON: It's my go.

NELSON picks up the dice.

CAROLINE: Arki, if I give you my two train stations, will you give me

the Electric Company, and Nelson Oxford Street, and Nelson, will you give me White Chapel, and I'll give you Bond Street?
ARKI: Say that again.
CAROLINE: I give you my train stations. You give me the Electric Company.
    You give Nelson Oxford Street, then he gives me White Chapel, and I give him Bond Street.
NELSON: I'm okay with that.
ARKI: That's a terrible deal Mum.
CAROLINE: For who?
ARKI: I'll have all four train stations, he'll have all the greens, you'll have those pissy little properties, Kent Road and the Water Works are mortgaged, and you've got no money.
CAROLINE: Okay I take it back.

    NELSON *rolls the dice.*

NELSON: Double six … Just get the HMAS Anaconda underway …

    NELSON *sails his warship twelve places around the table.*

SCENE TWELVE

AARON *is causing a scene at Caroline's gym.*

AARON: I've done nothing wrong! For Christ's sake.
CAROLINE: Calm down.
AARON: I could charge that old bag with assault. I was just sitting at the machine, I was just sitting there, totally minding my own business!
CAROLINE: You have to calm down or I will call the police.
AARON: Go ahead. Call the police. I am a member here. I have been a member here for years.
CAROLINE: I don't recognise you.
AARON: Yeah well I've been away. I suspended my membership. But I'm still a member. You ask anyone. You ask … what's his name, the bald one. The big bald guy.
CAROLINE: Gary?
AARON: Yeah Gary. You ask Gary.
CAROLINE: I'm not doubting you're a member. But you are not allowed to scream at people.

AARON: I wasn't screaming.
CAROLINE: That's what it sounded like.
AARON: This is outrageous.
CAROLINE: Calm down.
AARON: Yeah, well she manhandled me. That bloody old granny. She pulled my hand off the machine.
CAROLINE: She says she asked you first.
AARON: No she didn't. There was no please. She just pulled my arm off. She could have hurt me.
CAROLINE: She's nearly eighty. How is she going to hurt you?
AARON: What's she doing in a gym if she's nearly eighty?
CAROLINE: That's a really old-fashioned question. If you don't mind me saying.

> AARON *says nothing.*

Now, you had been on the same machine, the water winder, for an hour and forty-seven minutes.
AARON: It wasn't that long.
CAROLINE: It was that long. The equipment records how long you are on, and you were on that long. And that machine is part of a lot of people's circuits. There were fourteen people waiting to use the water winder—
AARON: [*muttering*] All geriatrics.
CAROLINE: Sorry?

> AARON *says nothing.*

It's a very popular item of equipment, and some people do like to stay on it a long time. That is why there is a sign on the water winder, saying that the most you can use it for is twenty minutes. Personally, I think twenty minutes is too long, but that was the decision made and that's the longest you are allowed to use it, so you can see why people were pissed off … cause you had been there an hour and forty seven minutes … On the same piece of equipment …

> AARON *feels a bit ashamed.*

AARON: I lost track of time.
CAROLINE: Okay.
AARON: I'm sorry.
CAROLINE: Okay. I'm not going to ban you. But I'm going to write this

down in the incident book, and if anything like this happens again, anything at all, you won't be able to come here.

    AARON *acquiesces silently.*

Alright.

    AARON *doesn't go.*

AARON: It's not easy for me you know.
CAROLINE: It's not easy for any of us.
AARON: Yeah but some of us have really good reasons for being a bit strung out you know, a bit on edge—
CAROLINE: I'm sure that's true. Let's just forget about it.
AARON: I have a nervous complaint.
CAROLINE: Okay.
AARON: I was in the Army … In Afghanistan.

    CAROLINE *stares at him, saying nothing.*

What are you looking at me like that for?
CAROLINE: You're a soldier?
AARON: That's what I said.
CAROLINE: And now you're … sick?
AARON: I don't know if I'd put it quite like that but, sure.
CAROLINE: Do you see …
AARON: What? Do I see what?
CAROLINE: Like … things that aren't there? Visions of people that you've killed … in the war …
AARON: That's a very personal question.
CAROLINE: I'm sorry.
AARON: How do you know I've killed anybody?
CAROLINE: I don't. I'm sorry … I didn't mean to offend you …

    AARON *looks very vulnerable all of a sudden.*

It's just … Are you busy this afternoon?

SCENE THIRTEEN

ARKI *and* AARON *sit on the couch at Arki's house.*

AARON: Do you get the shakes?
ARKI: Yep.

AARON: Hate that.

They sit in silence.

What drugs have they got you on?

ARKI: I'm not on any drugs. I'm doing behavioural therapy, and I'm doing lots of exercise.

AARON: That's good. Exercise is good. They all say that. Exercise a lot ... What sort of exercise do you do?

ARKI: Table tennis.

AARON: That's not really exercising.

ARKI: And I swim.

AARON: Okay ...

They sit in silence for a little.

I'm on Zoloft. It's an antidepressant. I get it sent direct from India. Cheaper than a chemist, and you don't have to go and see a shrink.

But listen, you're seeing a shrink, so you stick to the program.

ARKI: Does it work? Zoloft?

AARON: Sort of. Marijuana's better ... And scotch.

You really got it a bit young.

ARKI: They don't think I'm depressed. They think I'm more anxious.

AARON: Do you think you're depressed?

ARKI: I dunno.

AARON: Have you got a girlfriend?

ARKI: Nah ... What, you think if I got a girlfriend I'd be fine?

AARON: I didn't say that ... I didn't have a girlfriend at fifteen ... I think I had one at sixteen but.

ARKI: I'm not interested in girls.

AARON: Are you gay?

ARKI: No.

They are silent for a moment. CAROLINE *enters.*

CAROLINE: Milk?

AARON: Yeah, and two sugars.

She stands there for a moment, smiling uncertainly at them ... No-one talks ... She leaves them be.

Yeah ... well ... it's a fucker ...

He looks at ARKI. ARKI *smiles at him, shyly. He likes* AARON.

Least you're getting off school.
ARKI: I'm not. Today's a public holiday.
AARON: Oh yeah.
ARKI: Queen's Birthday.
AARON: Yeah, right.
ARKI: I've started playing the game again. The one I'm not meant to.
AARON: I have this stupid hankering to go back to Afghanistan. The place made me so sick, but I want to go back there. Offer me a ticket, I'd be straight on the plane. What's that about eh?

SCENE FOURTEEN

A misty strange landscape.

ARKI *stands, cold, in his pyjamas.* FIRST *and* SECOND MURDERER *enter.*

FIRST MURDERER: But who did bid thee join with us?

> ARKI *just looks at him.* SECOND MURDERER *prompts him.*

SECOND MURDERER: Macbeth.
ARKI: Macbeth.

> FIRST MURDERER *is not convinced.*

SECOND MURDERER: He need not our mistrust, since he delivers
  Our offices and what we have to do.
  To the direction just.
FIRST MURDERER: Then stand with us.

> *He gives* ARKI *a dagger. They all have daggers.*

  The west yet glimmers with some streaks of day;
  Now spurs the lated traveller apace
  To gain the timely inn, and near approaches
  The subject of our watch.

> *They both look at* ARKI *like he has forgotten his lines.*

ARKI: Hark! I hear horses.
BANQUO: [*off*] Give us a light there, ho!
SECOND MURDERER: Then 'tis he: the rest
  That are within the note of expectation
  Already are i' the court.

FIRST MURDERER: His horses go about.
It's your line Arki.
ARKI: I don't know it.
SECOND MURDERER: A light. A light.
ARKI: A light.

> BANQUO *and* FLEANCE *enter.*
>
> SECOND MURDERER *prompts* ARKI.

SECOND MURDERER: Tis he.
ARKI: No, but it's—
FIRST MURDERER: Stand to it.
ARKI: I can't. It's my psychiatrist and my—
BANQUO: It will be rain tonight.
FIRST MURDERER: Let it come down.

> FIRST *and* SECOND MURDERER *set upon* BANQUO, ARKI *follows suit.* FLEANCE *watches in horror.*

BANQUO: O, Treachery! Fly, good Fleance, fly, fly, fly!
Thou mayst revenge. O slave!

> ARKI, *his dagger and arm covered in blood looks at his mother. She flees.*

FIRST MURDERER: Let's away, and say how much is done.

> FIRST *and* SECOND MURDERER *exit.*
>
> ARKI *looks down at the body of Banquo.* BANQUO *slowly comes back to life.*

SCENE FIFTEEN

AARON *and* LILY *are at home. The sword now decorates the wall.*

AARON: You remember how I was really scared of the woman in the chemist?
LILY: Yeah.
AARON: I'm over that now.
LILY: That's great Aaron.
AARON: Now I'm scared of the guy in the Seven-Eleven.
LILY: The Indian guy?

AARON: Is he Indian?
LILY: The owner guy?
AARON: No, not the owner guy, the young guy. Big beard …
LILY: Oh yeah …
AARON: The one that chucks the all-nighters.
LILY: Do you want something? I can go.
AARON: No.

They say nothing for a moment.

When I ask for the smokes, they're in that black cupboard thing, you know, he takes them out really solemnly.
LILY: Maybe he's anti-smoking.
AARON: He never smiles at me.
LILY: He's probably just bored. That guy, he just looks like he doesn't want to be there.
What are you going to do today?
AARON: Oh I don't know …
LILY: I'll be going back to work in a few weeks.
AARON: I'll just stay here and look after Chloe.

LILY says nothing.

Or do a course … I don't know. Be a … I don't know. Plumber …

They say nothing for a moment.

LILY: I think you should see the army counsellor again.
AARON: I'm dealing with it myself.
LILY: Let them help you.
AARON: I know the drill. It's not rocket science.
LILY: It's the human brain. That's really complex, Aaron.
AARON: It's not that complex.
LILY: How can you say that?
AARON: It's just neurons and transmitters and shit, and cells and blood and muck … and a bit of dopamine, if you're lucky.

SCENE SIXTEEN

AARON *sits down, closes his eyes. A soothing, reassuring male American voice talks.*

VOICE: First find yourself a comfortable place to sit. It can be on a chair or on a cushion on the floor …

Silence.

Sit in an erect and dignified position. With a straight back. As still, as strong as a mountain.

Silence. AARON *sits, vulnerable, still.*

If you haven't already, and if you want to, you can shut your eyes, or concentrate on a spot on the wall or on the floor …

Silence.

You don't need to do anything. You don't need to go anywhere …

Now concentrate on the fact that you are breathing. Feel the breath as it goes in, and as it goes out. Feel it deep in the diaphragm, feel it as it enters the body, no need to interfere with it in any way …

AARON *switches off his phone and exits.*

SCENE SEVENTEEN

AARON *and* ARKI *are playing table tennis at Arki's house.* AARON *loses a point.*

AARON: What's the score?
ARKI: Eleven, sixteen.
AARON: Am I sixteen?
ARKI: No you're eleven. It's your serve.
AARON: I'm not eleven.
ARKI: Yeah, you're eleven.
AARON: There's no way I'm eleven.
ARKI: I've been counting.
AARON: You're sure it's me you're seeing, Arki. Me. Here.
Flesh and blood. Playing table tennis.

ARKI *laughs. They play a point.*

ARKI: Eleven, seventeen.

AARON: Let's start the game again. I vagued out. Completely vagued out. I'll serve.

He serves a fault.

Argh, I thought I was serving to that guy.

He points to an imaginary guy next to ARKI. ARKI *laughs.*

We are playing doubles?

They piss themselves laughing. ARKI *aces him.*

ARKI: Neither of you could get it.

They laugh.

Let's have a rally that goes on for hours and hours.

AARON: Okay.

ARKI: Let's play all night.

AARON: Don't know what your mum'll say.

ARKI: Let's go for the *Guinness World Records*.

AARON: How long do you have to rally for to get in the *Guinness World Records*?

ARKI: Eleven hours, fifty minutes and thirty-six seconds.

AARON: Is that right?

ARKI: Yeah, these two Australian guys did it.

AARON: Okay. If they can do it …

They rally for as long as they can, in silence.

The Zen of table tennis …

NELSON *enters, in uniform.* ARKI *and* AARON *look up.*

Sir.

ARKI: Um … this is Nelson. This is Aaron.

NELSON: You were in Afghanistan, Caroline tells me.

AARON: Yeah.

NELSON: What rank?

AARON: Lance Corporal.

NELSON: How many deployments?

AARON: Three.

NELSON: Which battalion? Sixth?

AARON: Seventh. I was at Base Ripley.
NELSON: Oruzgan.
AARON: Yeah.
NELSON: I know Captain Deveraux.
AARON: Yeah. Devo.

>AARON *sings a bit of the Devo hit—Whip It.*

NELSON: So what, you're on leave?
AARON: I'm ... um, non-effective at present sir.
NELSON: You alright Arki?
ARKI: Yep.
NELSON: Nice to meet you Aaron.
AARON: Yeah ... nice to meet you.

>NELSON *exits.*

Arki. Is that your dad?
ARKI: Nah ... He's a friend of my mum's.
AARON: Oh yeah.
ARKI: He's okay.

>AARON *doesn't say anything.*

He wants to take me to see the drone program.
AARON: What drone program?
ARKI: It's up in Queensland.
AARON: I didn't know we had a drone program.
ARKI: Well that's what Nelson says. We're going to drive up and see Dreamworld and all that stuff as well.
AARON: That sounds okay.
ARKI: He thinks he can cure me.
AARON: Cure you? There's no cure for this, mate.

>ARKI *looks crestfallen.*

Oh look, I dunno. Maybe there is. Why not. Give it a go.
ARKI: Do you want to come with us?
AARON: I don't think so.
ARKI: You could relax a bit. Have a holiday.
AARON: Do I look like I need a holiday?
ARKI: It's just for four days. Fly up Monday, fly back Friday.
AARON: That's five days mate. Four nights. Five days.

SCENE EIGHTEEN

Lily and Aaron's house.

LILY: Hasn't he got family?
AARON: Yeah. He's got family.
LILY: Why can't they look after him?
AARON: They do look after him.
LILY: What does he need you for?
AARON: What's the big problem?
LILY: I just don't understand why you're going.
AARON: I like him.
LILY: Sure, but—
AARON: And he's … sort of taken a shine to me.

    Pause.

  I'll only be gone a couple of days.
LILY: I worry about you.
AARON: Look maybe it's good we get a bit of a break.
LILY: You want a break.
AARON: I didn't mean it like that.
LILY: You want a fucking break?
AARON: I said I didn't mean it like that. Why don't you come? Bring Chloe.
LILY: I can't. I've got work.
AARON: I gotta go.

    He leaves. LILY *sits on the couch. Preoccupied. Upset. Her phone rings.*

LILY: [*into phone*] Hello.

    SAYF *and* NADIA *appear in the space,* SAYF *is on his mobile.*

SAYF: [*into phone*] Hello.
LILY: Can I help you?
SAYF: I'm the owner of Nights in Kabul.
NADIA: Co-owner.
LILY: Oh yes.

SAYF: You dined with us on the twelfth.
LILY: Yes.
SAYF: You, and your—
LILY: Husband.

>SAYF *hesitates.* NADIA *motions for him to get to the point.*

Did you happen to ... see a sword that was hanging next you on the wall?
LILY: Um ... Maybe ... I can't remember.

>*She looks guiltily round at the wall. The sword is gone.*

SAYF: It's gone. It disappeared ... that night.
LILY: Oh that's terrible ...
SAYF: It's real, you know. It's not a fake, it's a real heirloom.
LILY: I'm sorry.
SAYF: Its loss is causing us great distress.
LILY: I'm sorry. I am so very sorry that happened ...
SAYF: Did you take it?
LILY: No.
SAYF: Your husband. He didn't take it?
LILY: No.
SAYF: By accident ...
LILY: No.
SAYF: You're sure? You're sure you didn't take it?
LILY: Yes.
SAYF: Cause it was right by your table, it was right next to your table.
LILY: I'm—
SAYF: Cause it was there when you were eating, and then when you were gone, so was it. So you can see why—
LILY: We didn't take it. I'm sorry.

>LILY *hangs up.*

SCENE NINETEEN

NELSON *talks to* CAROLINE, ARKI *and* AARON *outside a highly secret defence base in Queensland.* NELSON *has a box of Krispy Kreme doughnuts.* AARON *carries an extremely long, thin bag.*

NELSON: Okay, now you have to remember that this is a huge privilege to be here. This is a highly secure, secret facility … Not even the Queensland Government knows exactly what goes on here.
AARON: What does go on here?
NELSON: I just said it was a secret, mate.
AARON: Sure, but—
NELSON: You know what a secret is?
AARON: Yeah, I know what a secret is.
NELSON: Why do I get the feeling I can't trust you, Aaron?
AARON: I just asked what goes on here. You said even the government doesn't know what goes on here—
NELSON: I said the Queensland Government.
AARON: Whatever. I was just asking—
CAROLINE: Calm down, Aaron.
AARON: What did I do?
NELSON: What are you even doing here?
CAROLINE: Arki wants Aaron to be here.
NELSON: Fine. Fine.
AARON: Do you know what your problem is?
NELSON: No, what is my problem?
AARON: Shell shock mate. Bomb fatigue.
NELSON: Bullshit.
AARON: I'm telling you, you've got all the—
NELSON: Shut the fuck up!
AARON: Uncontrolled anger. Irritability. Like all of us mate, fucked in the head.
CAROLINE: Stop bickering. Both of you. And stop swearing.
NELSON: Where did you get this idea Caroline, that you don't swear, and everybody else does. You swear like a bloody trooper.

Everyone is silent for a moment.

Colonel Boder from Nebraska runs the joint operation. He's a very good mate of mine. I knew him in Iraq, and he's pulled some strings for us. Now, just between you and me, he had a cousin who fought in Desert Storm, and very sadly … ended his own life.

CAROLINE, ARKI *and* AARON *listen bleakly.*

So he's very sympathetic … Now we won't be let into any of the operational areas, naturally, but I have arranged for Arki to meet a young woman that works on the computers, and she's happy to talk to Arki about the work she does, and how she feels about it. I've assured them we're not journalists, and I've explained about Arki being sick—

CAROLINE: And Aaron.

NELSON: No, I haven't actually mentioned Aaron being sick.

AARON: That's fine. I don't want to be mentioned.

CAROLINE: Why can't we say that Aaron's got a problem as well?

NELSON: I don't think there should be too many sick people in the party.

CAROLINE: Why not?

NELSON: For Christ's sake, we'll look like we're on a day leave from a psychiatric ward.

CAROLINE: That's offensive.

AARON: I'm not offended.

NELSON: I just meant—

ARKI: Look can we just go in and get it over with? Then we can go to Dreamworld.

Pause.

NELSON: What's with the bag?

AARON: My fishing rods.

NELSON: Yeah, well leave them in the hire car will you?

SCENE TWENTY

ARKI *is with* CONNIE *in the 'mess'. She is a young Australian soldier. Eighteen years old. She is eating a Krispy Kreme doughnut.*

CONNIE: What's wrong with you exactly?

ARKI: Um … well I used to play a lot of *Combat Mission*.

CONNIE: Awesome game.

ARKI: Yeah.

CONNIE: Did you play online?

ARKI: Yeah.

CONNIE: What was your username?

ARKI: Arkithirteen.

CONNIE: Arkithirteen … that rings a bell.

She looks at ARKI *speculatively.*

I'm Bella Swan seven nine six, like in *Twilight* ... so what happened to you?
ARKI: Well ... I just started playing a bit much, and Mum got worried.
CONNIE: Right.
ARKI: Sleep got a bit affected, that sort of stuff ...
CONNIE: Nasty. I'm glad it's that though, cause when they said you were sick, I thought you were like one of those kids with a really bad cancer ... So ... um, what can I tell you?
ARKI: Well, what do you do, exactly?
CONNIE: Mainly I'm sitting watching a screen, four hours on, two hours off. You need nice long breaks, cause your eyes get really tired and you've got to take breaks. Well you'd know that eh? And yeah, I'm just watching for any activity that might constitute insurgency. Like my UAV, I hate the word drone, by the way, I don't use it, none of us do.

ARKI *nods.*

In my opinion it's a racist word, even though strictly speaking they're not a race.
ARKI: It was always a total insult in *Star Wars*.
CONNIE: Totally.
ARKI: Not so much when Leia and Luke said it, but when Han Solo said it.
CONNIE: Wasn't that droid?
ARKI: Oh yeah, droid. Sorry.
CONNIE: Same dif. Droid. Drone. The implication is that AI is inferior.
ARKI: Yeah.
CONNIE: Anyway, so my reaper is flying over, I won't say what area cause that's like classified information.
ARKI: Right. Wow.
CONNIE: And I have to watch for any weapons, any suspicious activity, any mucking around by the side of the road, stuff like that, that might be their guys laying an IED, any suspicious vehicles, any gatherings that might amount to a threat to our troops on the ground.

She smiles at him.

ARKI: That's wild.
CONNIE: Luckily, you get like a sixth sense about whether something is

innocent or if it's suspicious, because you need to make split second decisions and sometimes the vision is really pixelated.

>ARKI *nods. He's a bit in awe of her.*

It's scary stuff, that's for sure. You get checked by the psych doctors every six months and you can go and talk to them whenever you want to. So far, I'm just above the average percentile for anxiety and depression. Which I blame not so much on my job, but more on a natural propensity I have to worry. I use natural remedies like chamomile, St John's wort, and valerian tea, and I sleep okay. Most of the time. I have the odd bad night, when I toss and turn, and I just get up, and drink the stress relieving tea that my sister sends me, she's a qualified naturopath and that's been a godsend … How old are you?

ARKI: Sixteen.

>*They sit in silence for a moment.* CONNIE *smiles at* ARKI.

So what do you do if you see something suspicious?

CONNIE: You tell the Americans. They're based in Houston. You know like 'Houston, we have a problem', yeah well they're there. You talk to them. And they look at the vision. And they decide if it's actionable, and if it's actionable, they take action.

>*Pause.*

[*Making a bomb sound*] Pchroouugh …

>ARKI *nods.*

Come on, I want to show you something.

>*She gets up and walks off.* ARKI *follows her.*

SCENE TWENTY-ONE

CONNIE *and* ARKI *are in Connie's bedroom.*

CONNIE: That's Anita's bed. She's the same as me, works with unmanned aerial vehicle predators … And this is my bed.

>CONNIE *smiles.* ARKI *looks away from the bed at her desktop computer.*

ARKI: Good gear.

CONNIE: Are you console or PC?

ARKI: I'm console but I'd be PC if I could afford it.
CONNIE: Watch this.

> CONNIE *logs on to something.* ARKI *watches … On the screen, we see what he is seeing. Drone footage.*

ARKI: Wow.

> *He takes it in.*

CONNIE: That's what I look at all day.
ARKI: You do it from your bedroom?
CONNIE: No … no.
ARKI: Are we hacking?
CONNIE: Nah.

> ARKI *laughs nervously. He looks back at the screen.*

ARKI: It's awesome.

> *The picture keeps moving, hovering over a small village.*

CONNIE: We're about twenty miles from a little village called Khost …

> ARKI *gazes at the screen.*

It's nine o'clock in the morning.

> *People are walking in a row.*

ARKI: So who's operating the …
CONNIE: Reaper …

> *She puts headphones on him.*

Here. You might hear them talking …

> ARKI *listens and watches.*

Like I said … boring.

> *Suddenly something is happening.*

ARKI: What's happening?

> *The people are bombed.*

Fuck.

> *He is glued to the screen. Another explosion happens.*

Fuck.
CONNIE: You alright mate?

ARKI *looks at her.*

I thought you'd like it.

ARKI *can't talk. He takes off the headphones.*

It's just a training video ... Aw shit.

ARKI *backs away and runs out of the room.*

SCENE TWENTY-TWO

SAYF *and* NADIA *are at the restaurant; it's after hours. They sit glumly.*

SAYF: Him I get. But her ... I don't see how she can let herself be a party to something like this.

NADIA *doesn't say anything. She is sick of the subject.*

Maybe they've fought about it. Maybe she told him he should bring it back to us, but he refused ...
Maybe he hits her.

NADIA: Why have you cast her as the nice one? She knows where we are. She could've brought it back. She's just as responsible for it as him. She might've been the one that took it in the first place.

SAYF: Why would she take it?

NADIA: She might be a kleptomaniac.

SAYF: No.

NADIA: She might have a house full of swords, and cups, and things she's stolen from restaurants ...

SAYF: I don't care which of them took it. I just want it back.

NADIA: What do you want a sword for anyway? A big bronze sword. You want to glorify war?

SAYF: No.

NADIA: You want to glorify death?

SAYF: No.

NADIA: You'd think you'd have had enough of war, but no, you hang a big macho bronze sword on the wall, you're an idiot. Forget about it now.

SAYF: I can't forget it.

NADIA: Hang something else up there.

SAYF: Every time I think about it, I feel insulted all over again. I feel a rage rising from the pit of my stomach, and it lodges in my chest, it

sits like a lead coffin in my chest. I can't bear they've got away with it.
NADIA: He was drunk. It was a meaningless, stupid act.
SAYF: No, you're wrong Nadia. He's sending us a signal.
NADIA: What signal?
SAYF: You have no right to be here. You don't deserve to own anything here. Anything you have, I can take, if I want.
NADIA: He's not that smart. He's just a dumb soldier, sent to our country, where he shouldn't have even been in the first place, taking it out on us, and pinching our sword.

Pause.

Have you thought maybe, that they didn't take it?
SAYF: Course they took it. Come on. I know they took it ... And we ring up and we're very friendly, and still they don't give it back.

Pause.

She liked the food didn't she?
NADIA: They ate everything.
SAYF: I think we should text her. Tell her that there is a special on at the restaurant ... A night of free food. For everyone.
NADIA: Why would we put on free food?
SAYF: I don't know ...
NADIA: You're getting too upset about this.
SAYF: Why shouldn't I be upset?
NADIA: I think you should go and talk to someone.
SAYF: No.
NADIA: A psychiatrist.
SAYF: No, no, I'm not going to do that.
NADIA: Maybe it's triggered things.
SAYF: Yes, it's triggered totally justifiable bloody rage.
NADIA: You were a boy soldier, little brother. You fought in the civil war when you were sixteen years old. Have you ever talked to anyone about that?
SAYF: You grew up in a war. Have you talked to anybody?
NADIA: No, but I didn't fight.
SAYF: So what? You saw terrible things. Terrible things happened to you. This isn't about us. It's about him. He stole something from us.

Pause.

NADIA: Maybe you should go and talk to the police.
SAYF: Are you kidding Nadia? I tell the police that I own this great big sword, they'll arrest me as a terrorist, and you'll never see me again. Where's my phone. I'm going to text her …

He starts texting.

NADIA: What are you going to say?
SAYF: I am going to say 'Return our sword or else.'
NADIA: I don't think we should threaten them.
SAYF: Why not. It was an aggressive act. By the Aussie soldier.
NADIA: I know, but—
SAYF: Alright I will say 'Return our sword or we will be sad for ever.'
NADIA: That's pathetic.
SAYF: Why can't we make an appeal to their heart?
NADIA: You've done that already. It didn't work.
SAYF: Do you think you would have done it any better?
NADIA: I can call her if you like.
SAYF: She's not answering her phone anymore.
NADIA: I could leave a message.
SAYF: I think a text is better … Return our sword, or you will regret it for ever.

NADIA is not impressed.

Return our sword, or you will remain barren.
NADIA: They've got a baby. I heard her talking about it.
SAYF: Could you please take the trouble to return our sword to us.
NADIA: I think you have to forget the sword, and move on …
SAYF: I can't.
NADIA: What about if I bought you a new one? Exactly identical?
SAYF: I told you. It's very old and precious. You wouldn't be able to find one the same.
NADIA: Have you looked on eBay?
SAYF: I don't want to look on eBay. I want my sword back. The one that was hanging on my wall.
NADIA: I'm sick of your sword. Why have you become so obsessed about your stupid sword? You never even mentioned the sword before this. Now it's your most precious possession. Every night. Every night we talk about the sword.

SCENE TWENTY-THREE

ARKI *lies quietly on his bed on the floor in Queensland. It's dark. His head is full of ghoulish images. He can't sleep.*

AARON *enters, trying to be quiet.*

ARKI: I'm awake.
AARON: Shit.

>*He laughs.*
>
>Are you alright?
>
>>ARKI *says nothing.*
>
>Not really huh …
>
>>AARON *gets out a cigarette and flicks his lighter.*

ARKI: Are you smoking?
AARON: Nup.
ARKI: You smoke in bed?
AARON: Nup.
ARKI: That's revolting.
AARON: Do you think your mother's going to marry Nelson?
ARKI: I dunno …

>ARKI *gets up and sits on Aaron's bed.*
>
>Why have you got your fishing rods in bed?

AARON: Safekeeping …

>ARKI *unzips the bag. He gets out the sword.*

ARKI: Wow … It's fantastic …

>ARKI *wields the sword, imagining terrible enemies.*
>
>Did you bring it back with you? From Afghanistan?

AARON: Yeah …

>If Nelson does marry your mother, don't you let him persuade you to join the Army, okay?

ARKI: They wouldn't let me in anyway, would they? They'd do a psychiatric assessment and I'd fail.
AARON: You sound a bit disappointed.

ARKI: No I'm not. I don't think I am.

AARON: Listen buddy. I don't think you're sick. I think you're on the money.

ARKI *scoffs*.

No I do. I think you're like ... now this is going to sound a little weird, I think you're like litmus paper. Dip you in something horrible and you turn blue. But you got to brush it off now. It's not gone in deep, it's surface shit man.

They are quiet a moment.

Let's get some sleep.

AARON *takes the sword from* ARKI.

ARKI: Aaron?
AARON: Yep?
ARKI: You're not going to commit hari-kiri?
AARON: Hurry curry ... No, I'm not.

SCENE TWENTY-FOUR

It's pizza night at Caroline and Archie's house with CAROLINE, LILY, AARON *and* NELSON. *They have names stuck to their foreheads.* NELSON *has Hilary Clinton.* CAROLINE *has John Wayne.* LILY *has Florence Nightingale, and* AARON *has Roger Federer.*

NELSON: Am I Cleopatra?
LILY, AARON and CAROLINE: No.
CAROLINE: Am I a man?
LILY, AARON and NELSON: Yes.
CAROLINE: Alive?
LILY, AARON and NELSON: Dead.
LILY: Am I a man?
AARON, CAROLINE and NELSON: No.
CAROLINE: Aaron.
AARON: Am I a cartoon character?
CAROLINE: No, you're real.
NELSON: Am I a man?
LILY, AARON and CAROLINE: No.

CAROLINE: Am I a sportsman?
LILY, AARON and NELSON: No.
LILY: Am I a rock star?
AARON, CAROLINE and NELSON: No.
NELSON: Am I Lady Godiva?
LILY, AARON and CAROLINE: No.
CAROLINE: Why are you thinking about Lady Godiva?
NELSON: I don't know. Famous woman.
CAROLINE: Famous naked woman on a horse.
NELSON: It's your go.
CAROLINE: Am I a film star?
LILY, AARON and NELSON: Yes.
CAROLINE: George Clooney?
LILY, AARON and NELSON: No.
LILY: My go. Am I dead?
AARON, CAROLINE and NELSON: Yes.
LILY: Am I Queen Elizabeth the First?
AARON, CAROLINE and NELSON: No.

> AARON *pauses before his go.*

CAROLINE: Come on Aaron.
AARON: Am I a war criminal?
LILY, CAROLINE and NELSON: No.

> LILY *gives him a sidelong glance.* ARKI *wanders in.*

CAROLINE: You want some more pizza mate?
ARKI: Thanks.

> ARKI *takes some pizza.*

NELSON: Am I Boudica?
LILY, AARON and CAROLINE: No.
CAROLINE: Am I John Wayne?
LILY, AARON and NELSON: Yes.
CAROLINE: I win!
ARKI: Who's John Wayne?
NELSON: [*to Arki*] Oh Arki. I will get you a copy of *The Green Berets*.
It is, without doubt, one of the finest examples of a soldier on film.
AARON: Bullshit.

NELSON: Have you seen it?
AARON: Nup.
NELSON: Well how would you know?
AARON: The guy never even fought in a fucking war.
NELSON: Who would you choose?
AARON: Not John Wayne.
NELSON: Who then?
AARON: It depends what you're going for, doesn't it?
NELSON: Reality. What it's really like to be in combat.
AARON: *Rambo.*
CAROLINE: Seriously?
AARON: Seriously ... Goldie Hawn in *Private Benjamin.*
LILY: I'd choose Ewan Macgregor in—what was it?
AARON: *Black Hawk Down.*
CAROLINE: He wouldn't be my top pick.
NELSON: I didn't know you liked war movies.
CAROLINE: I love a good war movie.

> ARKI *looks at his mum, thinking she's a bit of a hypocrite, but she hasn't noticed.*

I'm going to go Tom Hanks in *Saving Private Ryan.*
NELSON: That's an incredible movie.
CAROLINE: It's so real, and so graphic, the sound ... you feel like you're there. Fighting in a war.
ARKI: Sort of ... immersive. Like a video game.

> CAROLINE *gives him a look.*

NELSON: You might think it's Hollywood bullshit, but there are lots of guys in the Army who revere John Wayne.
CAROLINE: I get that. He's got this absolute unshakeable, I don't know, just calm, cool ...
AARON: Sure.
CAROLINE: I mean, isn't that what you need in battle?
AARON: I guess.
CAROLINE: Well you know, though, don't you Aaron? You've been in battle. You know.
AARON: I didn't meet many people like John Wayne there.
NELSON: I'll tell you something Boder told me. They are working on

a drug that can artificially create that sort of mental toughness in a person. Drugs that can neutralise any sort of nervousness or anxiety. Soldiers will be able to just pop a pill, and they'll be John Wayne.

LILY: That's terrible.

NELSON: Why?

LILY: They'll have no conscience.

NELSON: Who says they won't have a conscience?

Listen, it's a war. You don't want to do it badly. You don't want bad soldiers.

AARON: And anyway, you don't need drugs to have no conscience. You get trained to think the enemy isn't even human.

NELSON: Jesus Aaron, sometimes you spout some anti-war bullshit.

AARON: That's because I'm anti-war.

NELSON: That's just a symptom of your PTSD.

AARON: Piss off.

CAROLINE: We all hate war Aaron.

AARON: The only things drugs would do is make you less scared. That's what you're talking about isn't it? Drugs so you won't be so fucking scared.

Everyone is quiet for a moment. ARKI *slips away.*

CAROLINE: Whose go is it?

LILY: It's my go.

Am I Queen Victoria?

AARON: No. You're Florence fucking Nightingale … I'm sorry. I'm sick of this game.

He pulls off his slip of paper.

CAROLINE: That's a beautiful necklace Lily.

LILY: Aaron brought it back for me. It's very old. These little filigree bits, and the coins, and the little turquoise inlays. They were all used hundreds of years ago.

AARON: I hate to disappoint you Lil, but it's just a copy.

NELSON: Where'd you get it?

AARON: A guy on the Kandahar boardwalk.

NELSON: Looks pretty authentic.

AARON: Well it's not.

They are all silent a moment.

LILY: I love it. I don't care if it's not real. I love it.

AARON *leaves the room.*

SCENE TWENTY-FIVE

ARKI *sits in his bedroom playing a videogame.* AARON *enters.*

AARON: What are you doing?
ARKI: Nothing.
AARON: I don't care if you're playing your game.
ARKI: I'm not.
AARON: What are you doing then?
ARKI: I'm playing a new game. It's pretty graphic but it's—
AARON: Tell your mum, mate, not me.

ARKI *starts playing his game again.* AARON *watches.*

Who's Bella Swan seven nine six …? She wants to talk to you.
ARKI: Don't worry about it.

AARON *starts crying.* ARKI *holds* AARON. AARON *can't stop crying.* CAROLINE *enters.*

CAROLINE: What's happened?
ARKI: I don't know.
CAROLINE: Go and get Lily.

ARKI *exits.*

LILY *enters. She goes to* AARON. CAROLINE *leaves.*

LILY: You'll be okay.
You'll be okay.
AARON: Your necklace. Your beautiful necklace …
LILY: What about it?
AARON: I stole it … I stole it on a house raid in Derapet. It was on a bedside table. I saw it lying there, and I thought you'd look really beautiful in it …
LILY: Aaron.
AARON: No that's a lie. That's a lie. That's a lie, Lily. She was wearing it.

LILY *holds him.*

SCENE TWENTY-SIX

AARON *and* LILY *are back at the restaurant, Nights in Kabul, with* ARKI. SAYF *and* NADIA *watch* AARON *as he retrieves their sword out of his bag and places it on a table.*

SAYF: You bought a bag for it?

No-one says anything. SAYF *goes to the sword and picks it up and inspects it.*

AARON: It's fine. You know. I haven't done anything to it … I haven't killed anyone with it.

SAYF *takes it out of its scabbard. It looks cruel and menacing.* SAYF *looks at* AARON. *He can't quite divest himself of his bitter feelings. He looks like he would like to thrust it in his stomach.*

NADIA: That sword belonged to his grandfather, who fought against the English at Rawalpindi. And his grandfather gave it in turn to his father, who was a commander in the Mujahadeen, and fought in the mountains, holding back the Red Army from Kabul … That is why we called the restaurant Nights in Kabul.

This is laying it on a bit too thick, even for SAYF.

AARON: Yeah I'm sorry about that …

There is a long pause.

It's a beautiful sword man.

Another long pause.

SAYF: Okay. I forgive you.

They say nothing for a moment.

LILY: I'm Lily.
SAYF: Hi Lily.
NADIA: Hi Lily.
AARON: This is Arki.
NADIA: Is he your little brother?
AARON: Yep. Sort of.
SAYF: Hi Arki. I'm Sayf.

NADIA: Sayf means sword. In Arabic.

> *Pause.*

AARON: I'm Aaron.
NADIA: I'm—
AARON: Nadia. I remember.
SAYF: You want a coffee?
AARON: Sure. Just a little one.
LILY: Thanks.
SAYF: Sit down. What about you, Arki? You want a lemonade?
ARKI: Yes thank you.

> AARON, LILY *and* ARKI *sit down.* SAYF *disappears out the back and returns with Arki's lemonade.*
>
> NADIA *brings out coffee.*

AARON: Thank you.
SAYF: Got to be careful of the caffeine …
AARON: Yeah. I sleep like shit.
SAYF: So do I.
NADIA: I sleep like shit too.
LILY: So do I.
ARKI: Me too.

THE END

www.currency.com.au

Visit Currency Press' website now to:

- Buy your books online
- Browse through our full list of titles, from plays to screenplays, books on theatre, film and music, and more
- Choose a play for your school or amateur performance group by cast size and gender
- Obtain information about performance rights
- Find out about theatre productions and other performing arts news across Australia
- For students, read our study guides
- For teachers, access syllabus and other relevant information
- Sign up for our email newsletter

The performing arts publisher

www.ingramcontent.com/pod-product-compliance
Lightning Source LLC
Chambersburg PA
CBHW050023090426
42734CB00021B/3395